PUZZLE TABLES™

by
Thomas C. O'Brien

Cuisenaire Company of America, Inc.
12 Church Street, New Rochelle, N.Y. 10805

INTRODUCTION

Addition and multiplication tables make up a major part of a child's elementary mathematics education. It is therefore appropriate that work with Puzzle Tables be a part of a child's early experience in mathematics. The thinking that Puzzle Tables calls for is BASIC.

Before beginning this book, review the contents chart on the next page. Puzzle Tables is divided into four levels of difficulty. Sections on addition, subtraction, and multiplication provide problems in all four difficulty levels. The sections involving mixed operations and function rules provide problems at the medium, hard, or challenging levels.

Arrows are used on the first page of each section to illustrate the steps students should take to solve each Puzzle Table. The procedure for completing each Puzzle Table is similar to the more familiar number table:

+	1	2	3	4	5	6	7	8	9
1	2	3	4	5	6	7	8	9	10
2	3	4	5	6	7	8	9	10	
3	4	5	6	7	8	9	10		
4	5	6	7	8	9	10			
5	6	7	8	9	10				
6	7	8	9	10					
7	8	9	10						
8	9	10							
9	10								

Completing each Puzzle Table in the "Easy" sections is done by combining numbers on the side with numbers on top, according to the indicated operation: 2 + 4 = 6; 2 + 5 = 7; 3 + 4 = 7; 3 + 5 = 8.

More difficult sections of Puzzle Tables place the ( ) inside and outside the tables:

Here, number patterns and the order in which the problems are solved become the key to solving each Puzzle Table: 4 - 1 = 3; 7 - 1 = 6; 4 - □ = 1. The answer is 3. Now the remaining problem: 7 - 3 = 4. What are the number patterns in the completed Puzzle Tables? The numbers decrease by 2 across, and increase by 3 down.

In working these Puzzle Tables, children should be encouraged to use all the equipment they can—counters, Cuisenaire® rods, and even hand-calculators. Much of what children learn comes from their actions on things and their thinking about these actions. Further, they should be encouraged to work aloud (quietly) in small groups. Much of what children learn, they learn from one another.

Thomas C. O'Brien

Content Coverage
and
Levels of Difficulty

	Easy	Medium	Hard	Challenging
Addition **15 pages**	Find sums and look for patterns, one-digit facts. **Pages 1, 2, 3**	Find sums and look for patterns, larger numbers. **Pages 4, 5** Fill in outside and inside numbers, easy starting points. **Pages 6, 7**	Find outside and inside numbers, more difficult starting points. **Pages 8, 9, 10, 11**	No outside numbers given; no possible answers; several possible answers. **Pages 12, 13, 14, 15**
Subtraction **12 pages**	Find differences and look for patterns, one-digit facts. **Pages 16, 17, 18**	Find outside and inside numbers, easy starting points. **Pages 19, 20, 21**	Find outside and inside numbers, more difficult starting points. **Pages 22, 23, 24**	No outside numbers given; no possible answers; several possible answers. **Pages 25, 26, 27**
Multiplication **12 pages**	Find products, one-digit facts. **Pages 28, 29, 30**	Find outside and inside numbers, easy starting points. **Pages 31, 32, 33**	Find outside and inside numbers, more difficult starting points. **Pages 34, 35, 36**	No outside numbers given; no possible answers; several possible answers. **Pages 37, 38, 39**
Mixed Operations **4 pages**		Find outside and inside numbers, easy starting points. **Pages 40, 41**	Find outside and inside numbers, more difficult starting points. **Pages 42, 43**	
Function Rules **4 pages**			Apply function rules to find inside numbers. **Pages 44, 45**	Apply function rules to final outside and inside numbers; find function rules. **Pages 46, 47**

Page 48: Puzzle Tables Master Sheet
Pages 49-60: Answers and Commentary

Fill in the missing numbers. What patterns do you see in the completed Puzzle Tables?

1)

+	1	3
2	3	5
5	6	◯

Think: 5 + 3 = ?

Number Patterns:
Across __Increase by 2__
Down __Increase by 3__

2)

+	2	5
1	3	◯
4	6	9

Think: 1 + 5 = ?

Number Patterns:
Across_____
Down_____

3)

+	2	4
1	3	5
6	◯	10

Number Patterns:
Across_____
Down_____

4)

+	5	6
4	◯	10
7	12	13

Number Patterns:
Across_____
Down_____

5)

+	3	7
3	6	10
6	◯	◯

Number Patterns:
Across_____
Down_____

6)

+	4	8
2	6	◯
5	9	◯

Number Patterns:
Across_____
Down_____

Fill in the missing numbers. What patterns do you see in the completed Puzzle Tables?

1)

+	3	5
1	4	◯
3	◯	◯

Number Patterns:
  Across_____
  Down_____

2)

+	4	6
3	◯	◯
6	◯	12

Number Patterns:
  Across_____
  Down_____

3)

+	3	7
4	◯	11
5	◯	◯

Number Patterns:
  Across_____
  Down_____

4)

+	2	5
2	◯	◯
6	8	◯

Number Patterns:
  Across_____
  Down_____

5)

+	2	3
7	◯	◯
8	◯	11

Number Patterns:
  Across_____
  Down_____

6)

+	3	4
6	9	◯
9	◯	◯

Number Patterns:
  Across_____
  Down_____

Puzzle Tables © 1980
Cuisenaire Company of America, Inc.

Fill in the missing numbers. What patterns do you see?

1)

+	5	6
4	◯	◯
6	◯	◯

Number Patterns:
Across_____
Down_____

2)

+	3	4
5	◯	◯
8	◯	◯

Number Patterns:
Across_____
Down_____

3)

+	4	7
2	◯	◯
7	◯	◯

Number Patterns:
Across_____
Down_____

4)

+	7	9
0	◯	◯
5	◯	◯

Number Patterns:
Across_____
Down_____

5)

+	8	9
4	◯	◯
7	◯	◯

Number Patterns:
Across_____
Down_____

6)

+	0	10
8	◯	◯
9	◯	◯

Number Patterns:
Across_____
Down_____

Fill in the missing numbers. What patterns do you see in the completed Puzzle Tables?

1)

+	10	11
7	◯	◯
9	◯	◯

Number Patterns:
   Across_____
   Down_____

2)

+	5	8
10	◯	◯
11	◯	◯

Number Patterns:
   Across_____
   Down_____

3)

+	6	7
10	◯	◯
12	◯	◯

Number Patterns:
   Across_____
   Down_____

4)

+	10	14
3	◯	◯
5	◯	◯

Number Patterns:
   Across_____
   Down_____

5)

+	2	3
3	◯	◯
13	◯	◯

Number Patterns:
   Across_____
   Down_____

6)

+	4	5
6	◯	◯
16	◯	◯

Number Patterns:
   Across_____
   Down_____

Page 4

Fill in the missing numbers. What patterns do you see?

1)

+	14	15
5	◯	◯
6	◯	◯

Number Patterns:
Across_____
Down_____

2)

+	7	9
19	◯	◯
20	◯	◯

Number Patterns:
Across_____
Down_____

3)

+	9	10
17	◯	◯
20	◯	◯

Number Patterns:
Across_____
Down_____

4)

+	10	11
10	◯	◯
11	◯	◯

Number Patterns:
Across_____
Down_____

5)

+	18	28
14	◯	◯
24	◯	◯

Number Patterns:
Across_____
Down_____

6)

+	13	23
8	◯	◯
38	◯	◯

Number Patterns:
Across_____
Down_____

Find the outside numbers first. Next find the inside numbers. What patterns do you notice in the completed Puzzle Tables?

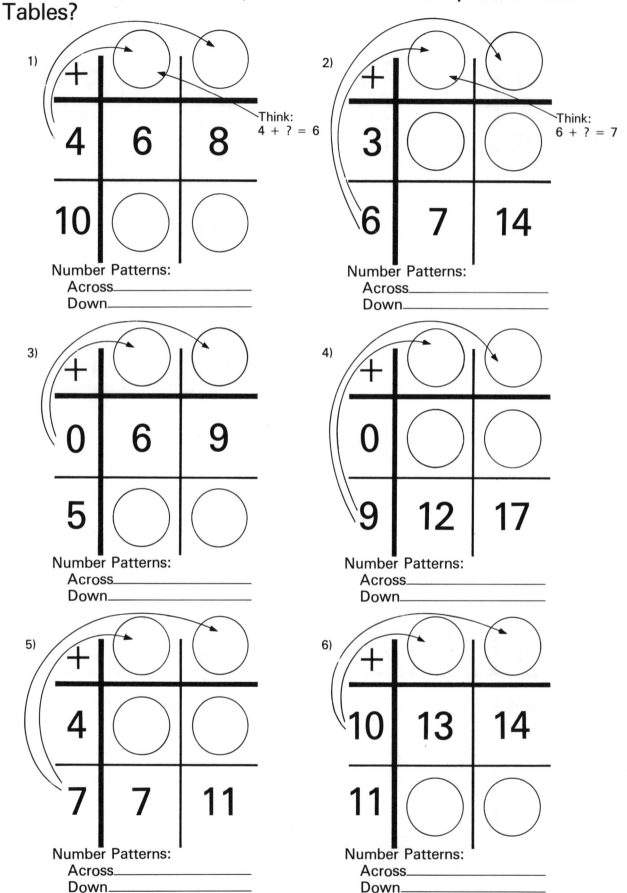

1)

+		
4	6	8
10		

Think: 4 + ? = 6

Number Patterns:
Across_____
Down_____

2)

+		
3		
6	7	14

Think: 6 + ? = 7

Number Patterns:
Across_____
Down_____

3)

+		
0	6	9
5		

Number Patterns:
Across_____
Down_____

4)

+		
0		
9	12	17

Number Patterns:
Across_____
Down_____

5)

+		
4		
7	7	11

Number Patterns:
Across_____
Down_____

6)

+		
10	13	14
11		

Number Patterns:
Across_____
Down_____

Page 6

Puzzle Tables © 1980
Cuisenaire Company of America, Inc.

Find the outside numbers first. Next find the inside numbers. What patterns do you notice?

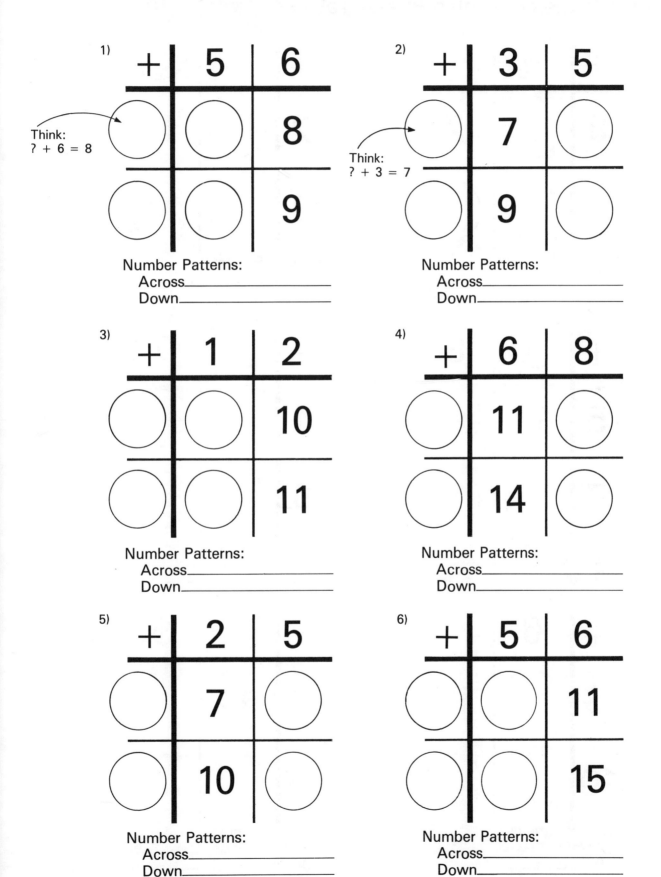

1)

+	5	6
○	○	8
○	○	9

Think:
? + 6 = 8

Number Patterns:
  Across_____
  Down_____

2)

+	3	5
○	7	○
○	9	○

Think:
? + 3 = 7

Number Patterns:
  Across_____
  Down_____

3)

+	1	2
○	○	10
○	○	11

Number Patterns:
  Across_____
  Down_____

4)

+	6	8
○	11	○
○	14	○

Number Patterns:
  Across_____
  Down_____

5)

+	2	5
○	7	○
○	10	○

Number Patterns:
  Across_____
  Down_____

6)

+	5	6
○	○	11
○	○	15

Number Patterns:
  Across_____
  Down_____

Find the outside and inside numbers. What patterns do you notice in the completed Puzzle Tables?

1)

+	5	◯
0	◯	7
2	◯	◯

Number Patterns:
Across_____
Down_____

2)

+	4	◯
2	◯	10
6	◯	◯

Number Patterns:
Across_____
Down_____

3)

+	◯	8
5	11	◯
7	◯	◯

Number Patterns:
Across_____
Down_____

4)

+	◯	7
4	9	◯
9	◯	◯

Number Patterns:
Across_____
Down_____

5)

+	6	◯
3	◯	12
10	◯	◯

Number Patterns:
Across_____
Down_____

6)

+	◯	9
7	11	◯
10	◯	◯

Number Patterns:
Across_____
Down_____

Puzzle Tables © 1980
Cuisenaire Company of America, Inc.

Find the outside and inside numbers. What patterns do you notice?

1)

+	5	9
◯	9	◯
7	◯	◯

Number Patterns:
Across_____
Down_____

2)

+	3	9
4	◯	◯
◯	12	◯

Number Patterns:
Across_____
Down_____

3)

+	3	5
◯	◯	10
7	◯	◯

Number Patterns:
Across_____
Down_____

4)

+	◯	9
2	◯	◯
◯	8	15

Number Patterns:
Across_____
Down_____

5)

+	◯	5
6	6	◯
9	◯	◯

Number Patterns:
Across_____
Down_____

6)

+	8	◯
7	◯	16
9	◯	◯

Number Patterns:
Across_____
Down_____

Puzzle Tables © 1980
Cuisenaire Company of America, Inc.

Find the outside and inside numbers. What patterns do you notice in the completed Puzzle Tables?

1)

+	◯	6
3	◯	◯
◯	9	11

Number Patterns:
Across_____
Down_____

2)

+	◯	4
◯	2	◯
7	8	◯

Number Patterns:
Across_____
Down_____

3)

+	◯	◯
◯	5	6
5	◯	9

Number Patterns:
Across_____
Down_____

4)

+	◯	3
◯	5	7
◯	9	◯

Number Patterns:
Across_____
Down_____

5)

+	◯	9
2	◯	◯
◯	8	15

Number Patterns:
Across_____
Down_____

6)

+	5	◯
◯	◯	10
◯	8	11

Number Patterns:
Across_____
Down_____

Puzzle Tables © 1980
Cuisenaire Company of America, Inc.

Find the outside and inside numbers. What patterns do you notice?

1)

+	4	◯
◯	9	15
◯	11	◯

Number Patterns:
Across_____
Down_____

2)

+	◯	8
6	◯	◯
◯	9	10

Number Patterns:
Across_____
Down_____

3)

+	◯	◯
1	◯	11
2	10	◯

Number Patterns:
Across_____
Down_____

4)

+	◯	7
◯	6	10
◯	◯	12

Number Patterns:
Across_____
Down_____

5)

+	8	◯
5	◯	21
◯	◯	31

Number Patterns:
Across_____
Down_____

6)

+	◯	◯
21	23	◯
31	◯	53

Number Patterns:
Across_____
Down_____

Even without knowing any of the outside numbers, you can still fill in the ◯ . Try it. There are many possible outside numbers for each of these. Record them on the blank Puzzle Tables Master Sheets.

1)

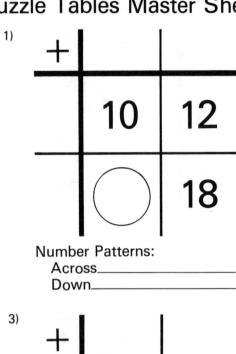

+		
	10	12
	◯	18

Number Patterns:
   Across_____
   Down_____

2)

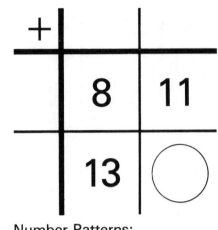

+		
	8	11
	13	◯

Number Patterns:
   Across_____
   Down_____

3)

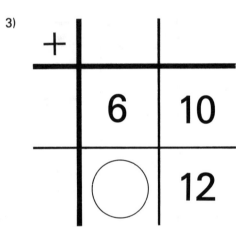

+		
	6	10
	◯	12

Number Patterns:
   Across_____
   Down_____

4)

+		
	9	◯
	15	19

Number Patterns:
   Across_____
   Down_____

5)

+		
	◯	14
	15	24

Number Patterns:
   Across_____
   Down_____

6)

+		
	20	24
	36	◯

Number Patterns:
   Across_____
   Down_____

Puzzle Tables © **1980**
Cuisenaire Company of America, Inc.

Each of these is impossible. Correct the Puzzle Tables to make them possible. Each of these can be made possible in more than one way. Record the corrections you would make on the blank Puzzle Tables Master Sheets.

1)

+	◯	◯
8	12	14
10	14	18

2)

+	◯	◯
◯	7	10
◯	9	11

3)

+	5	9
◯	11	15
◯	13	18

4)

+	4	7
◯	11	◯
◯	13	15

5)

+	◯	◯
◯	16	20
◯	21	27

Make an impossible one of your own.

6)

+		

These have several answers. Can you find them? Record your answers on the blank Puzzle Tables Master Sheets.

1)
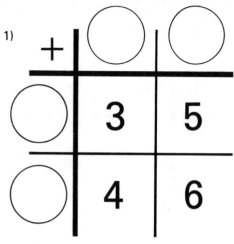

+	○	○
○	3	5
○	4	6

2)

+	3	○
7	○	○
8	○	○

3)

+	○	○
4	○	○
7	○	12

4)

+	○	○
○	4	6
○	10	12

5)

+	○	○
○	5	7
○	9	11

6)

Make up one of your own that has several answers.

Some of these are impossible. Some have several answers. Some can be answered in exactly one way. Which is which? Check the correct box. Show your answers.

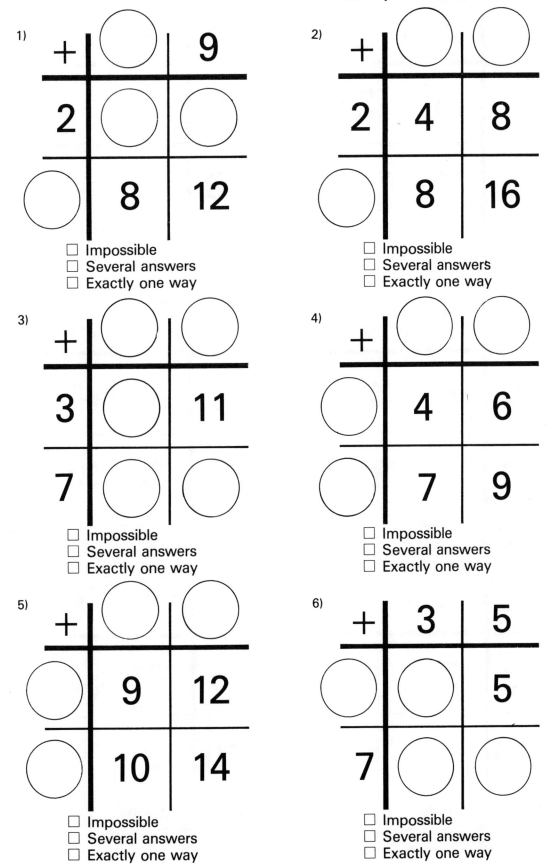

1)
+	◯	9
2	◯	◯
◯	8	12

☐ Impossible
☐ Several answers
☐ Exactly one way

2)
+	◯	◯
2	4	8
◯	8	16

☐ Impossible
☐ Several answers
☐ Exactly one way

3)
+	◯	◯
3	◯	11
7	◯	◯

☐ Impossible
☐ Several answers
☐ Exactly one way

4)
+	◯	◯
◯	4	6
◯	7	9

☐ Impossible
☐ Several answers
☐ Exactly one way

5)
+	◯	◯
◯	9	12
◯	10	14

☐ Impossible
☐ Several answers
☐ Exactly one way

6)
+	3	5
◯	◯	5
7	◯	◯

☐ Impossible
☐ Several answers
☐ Exactly one way

Fill in each missing number by subtracting the left number minus the top number. What patterns do you see in the completed Puzzle Tables?

1)

—	1	2
4	3	2
5	4	◯

Think: 5 − 2 = ?

Number Patterns:
Across _Decrease by 1_
Down _Increase by 1_

2)

—	3	4
6	3	◯
8	5	4

Think: 6 − 4 = ?

Number Patterns:
Across_____
Down_____

3)

—	1	5
7	6	2
9	◯	4

Number Patterns:
Across_____
Down_____

4)

—	2	4
5	◯	1
7	5	3

Number Patterns:
Across_____
Down_____

5)

—	6	7
8	2	1
10	◯	◯

Number Patterns:
Across_____
Down_____

6)

—	2	5
6	4	◯
10	8	◯

Number Patterns:
Across_____
Down_____

Puzzle Tables © 1980
Cuisenaire Company of America, Inc.

Fill in each missing number by subtracting the left number minus the top number. What patterns do you see in the completed Puzzle Tables?

1)

−	1	4
8	7	◯
10	◯	◯

Number Patterns:
Across‗‗‗‗‗‗‗‗‗‗
Down‗‗‗‗‗‗‗‗‗‗

2)

−	2	6
9	◯	◯
12	◯	6

Number Patterns:
Across‗‗‗‗‗‗‗‗‗‗
Down‗‗‗‗‗‗‗‗‗‗

3)

−	3	4
12	◯	8
14	◯	◯

Number Patterns:
Across‗‗‗‗‗‗‗‗‗‗
Down‗‗‗‗‗‗‗‗‗‗

4)

−	6	9
14	◯	◯
16	10	◯

Number Patterns:
Across‗‗‗‗‗‗‗‗‗‗
Down‗‗‗‗‗‗‗‗‗‗

5)

−	8	9
15	◯	◯
17	◯	8

Number Patterns:
Across‗‗‗‗‗‗‗‗‗‗
Down‗‗‗‗‗‗‗‗‗‗

6)

−	6	7
13	7	◯
15	◯	◯

Number Patterns:
Across‗‗‗‗‗‗‗‗‗‗
Down‗‗‗‗‗‗‗‗‗‗

Puzzle Tables © 1980
Cuisenaire Company of America, Inc.

Fill in each missing number by subtracting the left number minus the top number. What patterns do you see in the completed Puzzle Tables?

1)

—	4	7
11	◯	◯
15	◯	◯

Number Patterns:
Across_____
Down_____

2)

—	5	7
14	◯	◯
17	◯	◯

Number Patterns:
Across_____
Down_____

3)

—	5	9
9	◯	◯
19	◯	◯

Number Patterns:
Across_____
Down_____

4)

—	4	8
12	◯	◯
18	◯	◯

Number Patterns:
Across_____
Down_____

5)

—	7	8
10	◯	◯
16	◯	◯

Number Patterns:
Across_____
Down_____

6)

—	6	9
13	◯	◯
17	◯	◯

Number Patterns:
Across_____
Down_____

Page 18

Puzzle Tables © 1980
Cuisenaire Company of America, Inc.

Find the outside numbers first. Next find the inside numbers. What patterns do you notice?

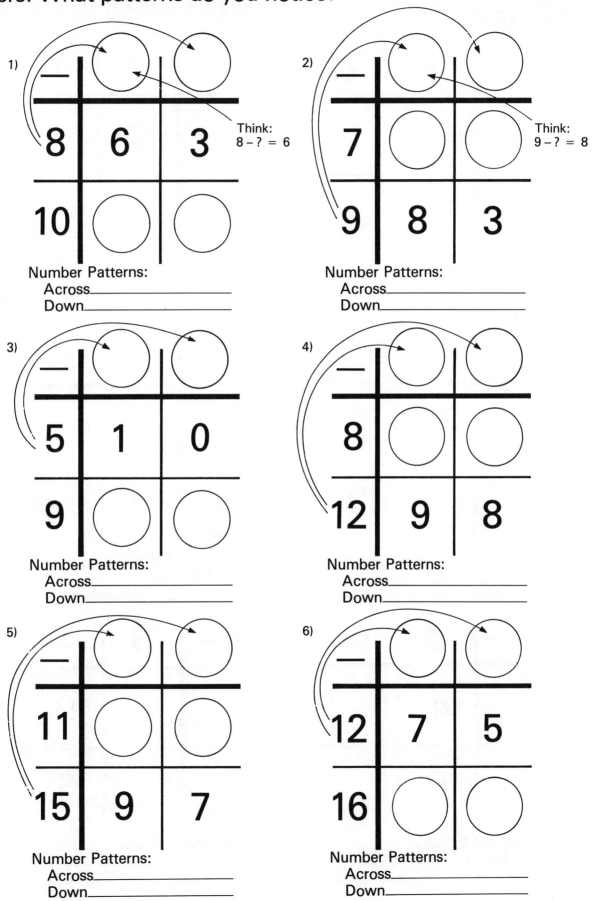

1)

8	6	3
10		

Think:
8 – ? = 6

Number Patterns:
Across_____
Down_____

2)

7		
9	8	3

Think:
9 – ? = 8

Number Patterns:
Across_____
Down_____

3)

5	1	0
9		

Number Patterns:
Across_____
Down_____

4)

8		
12	9	8

Number Patterns:
Across_____
Down_____

5)

11		
15	9	7

Number Patterns:
Across_____
Down_____

6)

12	7	5
16		

Number Patterns:
Across_____
Down_____

Find the outside numbers first. Next find the inside numbers. What patterns do you notice in the completed Puzzle Tables?

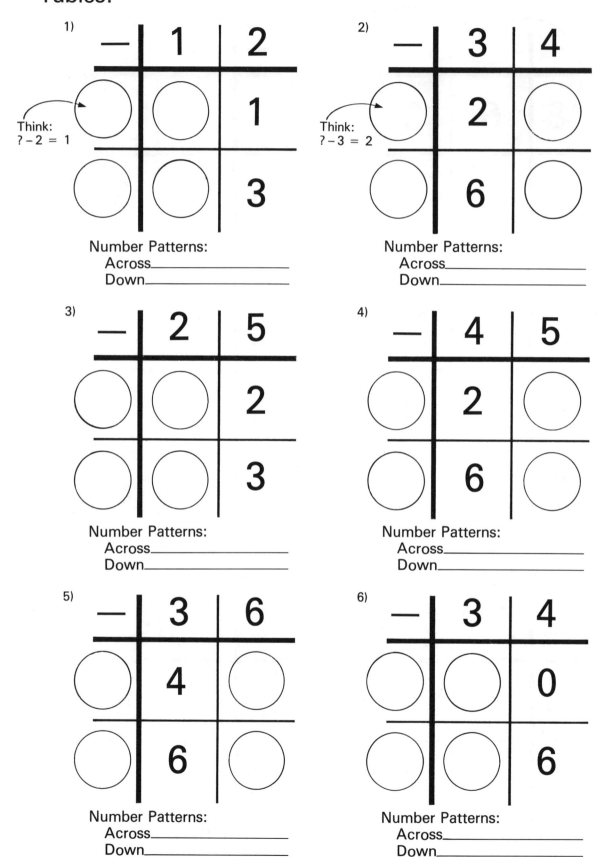

1)

−	1	2
○	○	1
○	○	3

Think:
? − 2 = 1

Number Patterns:
Across_____
Down_____

2)

−	3	4
○	2	○
○	6	○

Think:
? − 3 = 2

Number Patterns:
Across_____
Down_____

3)

−	2	5
○	○	2
○	○	3

Number Patterns:
Across_____
Down_____

4)

−	4	5
○	2	○
○	6	○

Number Patterns:
Across_____
Down_____

5)

−	3	6
○	4	○
○	6	○

Number Patterns:
Across_____
Down_____

6)

−	3	4
○	○	0
○	○	6

Number Patterns:
Across_____
Down_____

Page 20

Find the outside numbers first. Next find the inside numbers. What patterns do you notice?

1)

−	◯	◯
13	9	5
17	◯	◯

Number Patterns:
Across_____
Down_____

2)

−	7	9
◯	◯	7
◯	◯	9

Number Patterns:
Across_____
Down_____

3)

−	◯	◯
11	◯	◯
15	8	7

Number Patterns:
Across_____
Down_____

4)

−	8	9
◯	4	◯
◯	6	◯

Number Patterns:
Across_____
Down_____

5)

−	7	9
◯	◯	9
◯	◯	10

Number Patterns:
Across_____
Down_____

6)

−	◯	◯
14	8	6
16	◯	◯

Number Patterns:
Across_____
Down_____

Puzzle Tables © 1980
Cuisenaire Company of America, Inc.

Find the outside and inside numbers. What patterns do you notice in the completed Puzzle Tables?

1)

—	1	◯
4	◯	1
7	◯	◯

Number Patterns:
Across_____
Down_____

2)

—	0	◯
2	◯	1
6	◯	◯

Number Patterns:
Across_____
Down_____

3)

—	◯	1
5	5	◯
8	◯	◯

Number Patterns:
Across_____
Down_____

4)

—	◯	5
6	4	◯
7	◯	◯

Number Patterns:
Across_____
Down_____

5)

—	2	◯
5	◯	1
9	◯	◯

Number Patterns:
Across_____
Down_____

6)

—	◯	6
8	4	◯
10	◯	◯

Number Patterns:
Across_____
Down_____

Puzzle Tables © 1980
Cuisenaire Company of America, Inc.

Find the outside and inside numbers. What patterns do you notice?

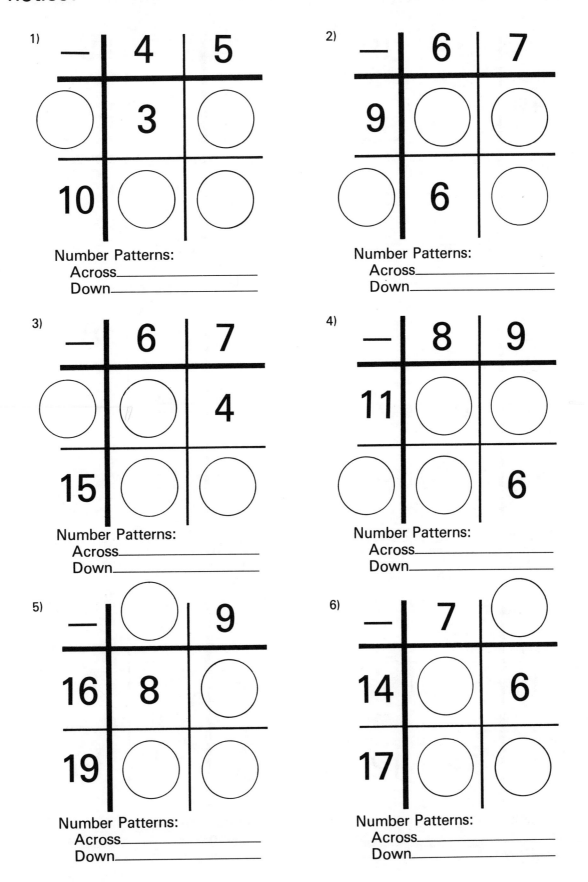

1)

—	4	5
◯	3	◯
10	◯	◯

Number Patterns:
Across_____
Down_____

2)

—	6	7
9	◯	◯
◯	6	◯

Number Patterns:
Across_____
Down_____

3)

—	6	7
◯	◯	4
15	◯	◯

Number Patterns:
Across_____
Down_____

4)

—	8	9
11	◯	◯
◯	◯	6

Number Patterns:
Across_____
Down_____

5)

—	◯	9
16	8	◯
19	◯	◯

Number Patterns:
Across_____
Down_____

6)

—	7	◯
14	◯	6
17	◯	◯

Number Patterns:
Across_____
Down_____

Puzzle Tables © 1980
Cuisenaire Company of America, Inc.

Find the outside and inside numbers. What patterns do you notice in the completed Puzzle Tables?

1)

	◯	8
11	◯	◯
◯	8	6

Number Patterns:
Across_____
Down_____

2)

	◯	9
◯	8	◯
19	12	◯

Number Patterns:
Across_____
Down_____

3)

	◯	◯
◯	8	7
16	◯	8

Number Patterns:
Across_____
Down_____

4)

	◯	8
◯	6	4
◯	11	◯

Number Patterns:
Across_____
Down_____

5)

	◯	7
11	◯	◯
◯	14	12

Number Patterns:
Across_____
Down_____

6)

	8	◯
◯	◯	9
◯	11	10

Number Patterns:
Across_____
Down_____

Puzzle Tables © 1980
Cuisenaire Company of America, Inc.

Even without knowing any of the outside numbers, you can still fill in the ◯ . Try it. There are many possible outside numbers for each of these. Record them on the blank Puzzle Tables Master Sheets.

1)

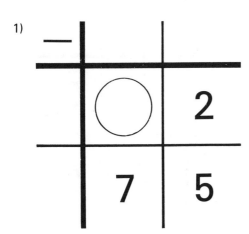

◯	2
7	5

2)

7	◯
9	6

3)

5	2
8	◯

4)

6	1
◯	5

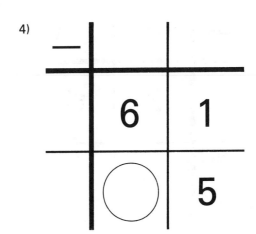

5)

6	◯
7	1

6)

◯	0
9	5

Puzzle Tables © 1980
Cuisenaire Company of America, Inc.

Each of these is impossible. Correct the Puzzle Tables to make them possible. Each of these can be made possible in more than one way. Record the corrections you would make on the blank Puzzle Tables Master Sheets.

1)

−	◯	◯
8	5	2
9	6	4

2)

−	◯	◯
◯	4	3
◯	7	4

3)

−	8	◯
◯	3	6
◯	9	5

4)

−	5	9
◯	6	1
◯	◯	4

5)

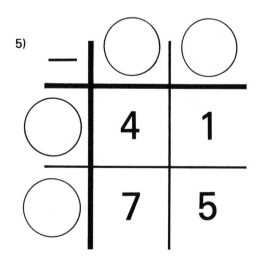

−	◯	◯
◯	4	1
◯	7	5

6)

Make an impossible one of your own.

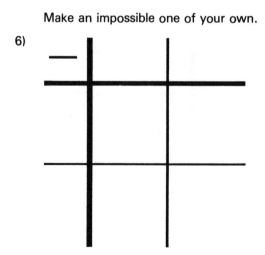

Puzzle Tables © 1980
Cuisenaire Company of America, Inc.

These have several answers. Can you find them? Record your answers on the blank Puzzle Tables Master Sheets.

1)

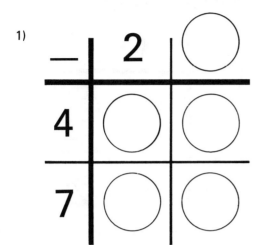

—	2	
4		
7		

2)

—		
	2	1
	3	2

3)

—		
	4	3
	6	5

4)

—		
10		
12		3

5)

—	7	9
		4

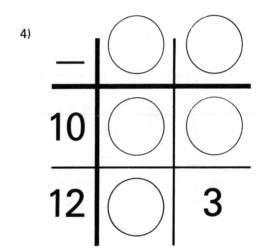

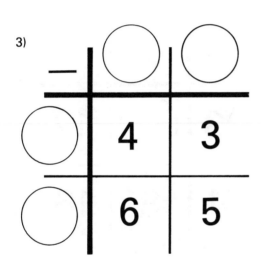

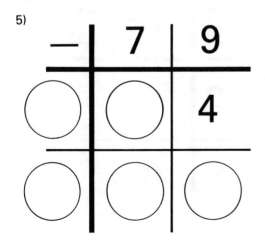

Make up one of your own that has several answers.

6)

—		

Puzzle Tables © 1980
Cuisenaire Company of America, Inc.

Fill in the missing numbers.

1)

x	2	5
1	2	5
3	6	◯

Think:
3 x 5 = ?

2)

x	1	4
2	2	◯
5	5	20

Think:
2 x 4 = ?

3)

x	3	5
2	6	10
4	◯	20

4)

x	2	4
3	◯	12
4	8	16

5)

x	3	5
3	9	15
5	◯	◯

6)

x	0	4
2	0	◯
5	0	◯

Puzzle Tables © 1980
Cuisenaire Company of America, Inc.

Fill in the missing numbers.

1)

x	5	6
2	10	◯
3	◯	◯

2)

x	7	9
4	◯	◯
5	◯	45

3)

x	7	8
3	◯	24
6	◯	◯

4)

x	8	9
2	◯	◯
5	40	◯

5)

x	4	6
1	◯	◯
7	◯	42

6)

x	4	6
6	24	◯
8	◯	◯

Fill in the missing numbers.

1)

x	6	7
6	◯	◯
8	◯	◯

2)

x	6	7
5	◯	◯
7	◯	◯

3)

x	8	9
5	◯	◯
6	◯	◯

4)

x	7	8
7	◯	◯
8	◯	◯

5)

x	7	10
6	◯	◯
9	◯	◯

6)

x	5	9
7	◯	◯
9	◯	◯

Puzzle Tables © 1980
Cuisenaire Company of America, Inc.

Find the outside numbers first. Next find the inside numbers.

1)

X	○	○
4	8	16
10	○	○

2)

X	○	○
3	○	○
6	6	48

3)

X	○	○
0	0	○
5	○	45

4)

X	○	○
8	○	○
10	40	60

5)

X	○	○
7	○	○
8	32	72

6)

X	○	○
2	14	20
10	○	○

Find the outside numbers first. Next find the inside numbers.

1)

x	5	6
○	○	12
○	○	18

Think:
? x 6 = 12

2)

x	3	5
○	12	○
○	18	○

Think:
? x 3 = 12

3)

x	1	2
○	○	16
○	○	18

4)

x	6	8
○	30	○
○	48	○

5)

x	2	5
○	10	○
○	16	○

6)

x	5	6
○	○	30
○	○	54

Puzzle Tables © 1980
Cuisenaire Company of America, Inc.

Find the outside numbers first. Next find the inside numbers.

1)

x	◯	◯
4	8	16
10	◯	◯

2)

x	1	8
◯	◯	24
◯	◯	48

3)

x	◯	◯
0	◯	◯
5	30	45

4)

x	3	8
◯	0	◯
◯	27	◯

5)

x	0	4
◯	◯	16
◯	◯	28

6)

x	◯	◯
9	27	36
10	◯	◯

Find the inside and outside numbers.

1)

x	4	◯
2	◯	16
6	◯	◯

2)

x	5	◯
0	◯	0
2	◯	◯

3)

x	◯	8
5	30	◯
7	◯	◯

4)

x	◯	7
4	20	◯
9	◯	◯

5)

x	6	◯
3	◯	27
10	◯	◯

6)

x	◯	9
7	28	◯
10	◯	◯

Puzzle Tables © 1980
Cuisenaire Company of America, Inc.

Find the inside and outside numbers.

1)

x	5	9
( )	20	( )
7	( )	( )

2)

x	3	9
4	( )	( )
( )	27	( )

3)

x	3	5
( )	( )	25
7	( )	( )

4)

x	2	9
2	( )	( )
( )	( )	54

5)

x	( )	5
6	0	( )
9	( )	( )

6)

x	8	( )
7	( )	63
9	( )	( )

Find the inside and outside numbers.

1)

x	◯	6
3	◯	◯
◯	20	30

2)

x	◯	4
◯	1	◯
7	7	◯

3)

x	◯	◯
◯	6	8
5	◯	20

4)

x	◯	3
◯	4	12
◯	8	◯

5)

x	◯	9
2	◯	◯
◯	12	54

6)

x	5	◯
◯	◯	16
◯	15	24

Even without knowing any of the outside numbers, you can still fill in the ◯ . Try it. There are many possible outside numbers for each of these. Record them on the blank Puzzle Tables Master Sheets.

1)

X		
	◯	18
	10	30

2)

X		
	12	◯
	27	63

3)

X		
	10	12
	15	◯

4)

X		
	20	25
	◯	50

5)

X		
	28	◯
	42	48

6)

X		
	◯	63
	48	72

Some of these are impossible. Some have several answers. Some can be answered in exactly one way. Which is which? Check the correct box. Show your answers.

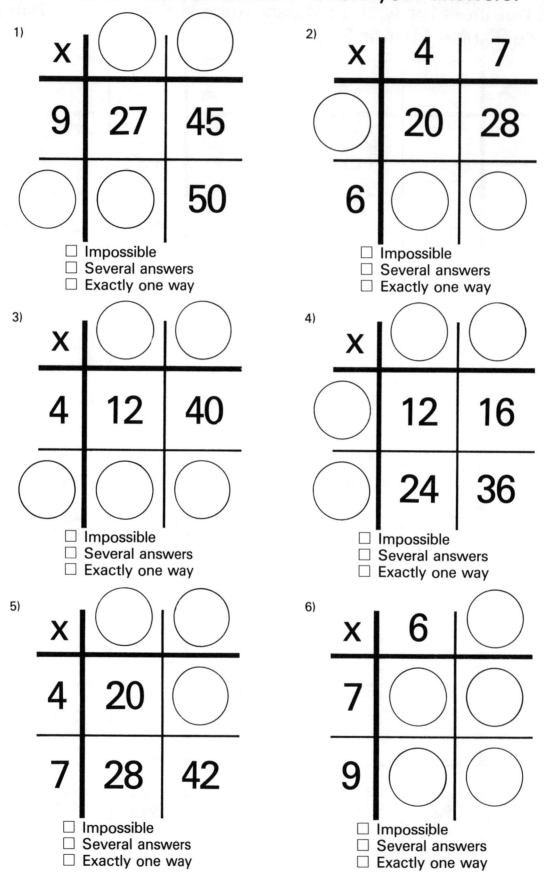

1)

x	◯	◯
9	27	45
◯	◯	50

☐ Impossible
☐ Several answers
☐ Exactly one way

2)

x	4	7
◯	20	28
6	◯	◯

☐ Impossible
☐ Several answers
☐ Exactly one way

3)

x	◯	◯
4	12	40
◯	◯	◯

☐ Impossible
☐ Several answers
☐ Exactly one way

4)

x	◯	◯
◯	12	16
◯	24	36

☐ Impossible
☐ Several answers
☐ Exactly one way

5)

x	◯	◯
4	20	◯
7	28	42

☐ Impossible
☐ Several answers
☐ Exactly one way

6)

x	6	◯
7	◯	◯
9	◯	◯

☐ Impossible
☐ Several answers
☐ Exactly one way

Page 38

Puzzle Tables © 1980
Cuisenaire Company of America, Inc.

Some of these are impossible. Some have several answers. Some can be answered in exactly one way. Which is which? Check the correct box. Show your answers.

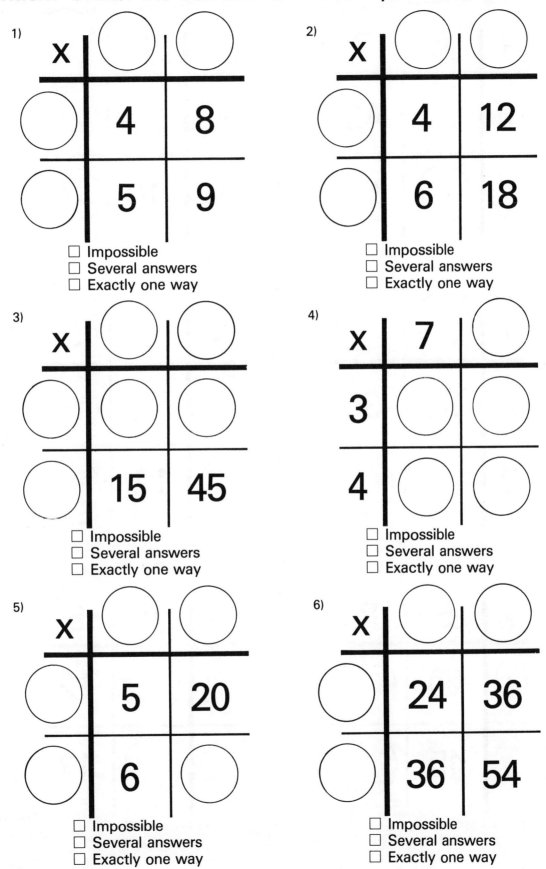

1)

X	◯	◯
◯	4	8
◯	5	9

☐ Impossible
☐ Several answers
☐ Exactly one way

2)

X	◯	◯
◯	4	12
◯	6	18

☐ Impossible
☐ Several answers
☐ Exactly one way

3)

X	◯	◯
◯	◯	◯
◯	15	45

☐ Impossible
☐ Several answers
☐ Exactly one way

4)

X	7	◯
3	◯	◯
4	◯	◯

☐ Impossible
☐ Several answers
☐ Exactly one way

5)

X	◯	◯
◯	5	20
◯	6	◯

☐ Impossible
☐ Several answers
☐ Exactly one way

6)

X	◯	◯
◯	24	36
◯	36	54

☐ Impossible
☐ Several answers
☐ Exactly one way

Puzzle Tables © 1980
Cuisenaire Company of America, Inc.

Fill in the missing numbers. Review the operations.

1)

+	6	7
◯	◯	12
◯	◯	14

2)

−	◯	◯
10	◯	◯
15	10	7

3)

x	◯	◯
5	30	35
7	◯	◯

4)

−	6	9
◯	7	◯
◯	12	◯

5)

x	5	8
◯	20	◯
◯	45	◯

6)

+	5	8
◯	◯	12
◯	◯	17

Puzzle Tables © 1980
Cuisenaire Company of America, Inc.

Fill in the missing numbers. Review the operations.

1)

×	7	9
◯	◯	54
◯	◯	72

2)

−	◯	◯
11	7	4
14	◯	◯

3)

+	7	9
◯	13	◯
◯	15	◯

4)

−	8	9
◯	◯	3
◯	◯	8

5)

+	◯	◯
5	13	14
8	◯	◯

6)

×	◯	◯
5	◯	◯
8	64	72

Fill in the missing numbers. Review the operations.

1)

−	3	7
◯	6	◯
11	◯	◯

2)

×	◯	7
3	◯	◯
8	48	◯

3)

+	1	◯
5	◯	9
9	◯	◯

4)

−	◯	9
11	3	◯
14	◯	◯

5)

×	◯	9
5	40	◯
6	◯	◯

6)

+	8	9
◯	◯	12
7	◯	◯

Puzzle Tables © 1980
Cuisenaire Company of America, Inc.

Fill in the missing numbers. Review the operations.

1)

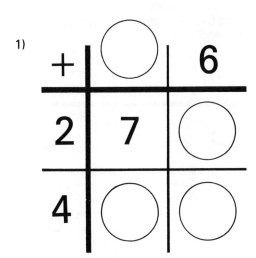

+	◯	6
2	7	◯
4	◯	◯

2)

x	3	7
4	◯	◯
◯	21	◯

3)

−	8	9
◯	◯	8
19	◯	◯

4)

+	3	7
6	◯	◯
◯	11	◯

5)

−	7	◯
16	◯	7
18	◯	◯

6)

x	8	9
◯	56	◯
8	◯	◯

Puzzle Tables © 1980
Cuisenaire Company of America, Inc.

Complete each function rule as indicated.

1) Multiply the left number times the top number and then add 2.

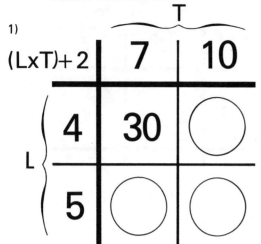

(LxT)+ 2	T 7	10
L 4	30	◯
5	◯	◯

2) Add the left number and the top number and then add 10.

(L+T)+10	3	6
4	◯	◯
7	◯	23

3) Multiply the left number times the top number and then subtract 5.

(LxT)-5	10	12
6	◯	◯
8	75	◯

4) Add the left number and the top number and then multiply the result by 2.

(L+T)x2	2	5
3	◯	◯
4	12	◯

5) Multiply 2 times the left number and then add the top number.

(2xL)+T	2	3
5	12	◯
9	◯	◯

6) Make up one of your own.

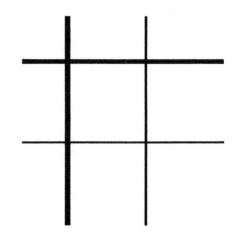

Puzzle Tables © 1980
Cuisenaire Company of America, Inc.

Complete each function rule as indicated. Describe the function rule in words using L (left number) and T (top number).

1) (L+T)x5

	3
○	○ 15
7 40	○

2) (LxT)+1

4	○
6 ○	43
○ 37	○

_____

_____

3) (L+2)+T

○	○
7 15	19
12 ○	○

4) (2xL)+T

2	4
○ ○	14
○ 16	○

_____

_____

5) (2xL)-T

○	4
5 8	○
○ ○	10

6) Make up one of your own.

_____

_____

Puzzle Tables © 1980
Cuisenaire Company of America, Inc.

Page 45

Complete each function rule as indicated. Describe the function rule in words using L (left number) and T (top number).

1)

$(L+T)-6$

	7	8
10	◯	◯
11	12	◯

_____

_____

2)

$(L+1) \times T$

	9	15
4	45	◯
5	◯	◯

_____

_____

3)

$(L+T)^2$

	4	10
3	49	◯
5	◯	◯

Think:
$(3+4)^2 =$
$7^2 = 7 \times 7$

_____

_____

4)

L^2+T

	4	10
6	◯	◯
7	53	◯

_____

_____

5)

$L+T^2$

	4	10
6	22	◯
7	◯	◯

_____

_____

6)

Make up one of your own.

_____

_____

Puzzle Tables © 1980
Cuisenaire Company of America, Inc.

What's been done to the left and top numbers? Write the function rules using L (left) and T (top).

1)

	9	11
4	18	20
5	19	21

_____

2)

	12	13
7	2	1
10	8	7

_____

3)

	5	7
0	5	7
3	11	13

_____

4)

	7	8
10	60	70
12	72	84

_____

5)

	4	7
8	16	22
9	17	23

_____

6)

Make up one of your own.

_____

Puzzle Tables Master Sheet

1)

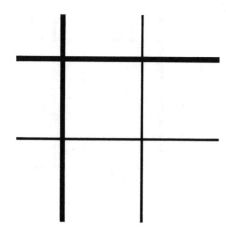

2)

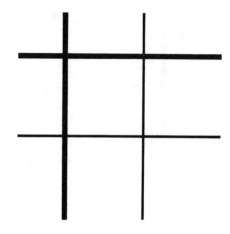

3)

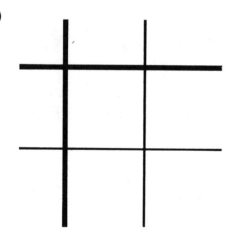

4)

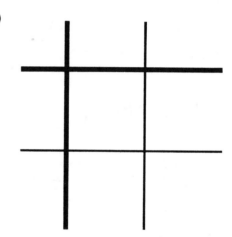

5)

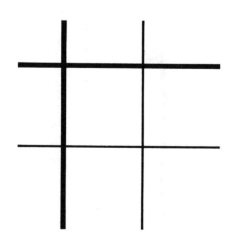

6)

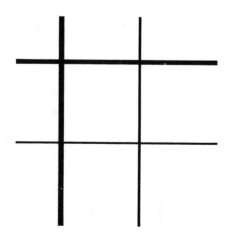

Teacher Notes: pages 1-4
  The inside numbers have the same pattern as the outside numbers, across and down.

Page 1

1)

+	1	3
2	3	5
5	6	(8)

2)

+	2	5
1	3	(6)
4	6	9

3)

+	2	4
1	3	5
6	(8)	10

4)

+	5	6
4	(9)	10
7	12	13

5)

+	3	7
3	6	10
6	(9)	(13)

6)

+	4	8
2	6	(10)
5	9	(13)

Page 2

1)

+	3	5
1	4	(6)
3	(6)	(8)

2)

+	4	6
3	(7)	(9)
6	(10)	12

3)

+	3	7
4	(7)	11
5	(8)	(12)

4)

+	2	5
2	(4)	(7)
6	8	(11)

5)

+	2	3
7	(9)	(10)
8	(10)	11

6)

+	3	4
6	9	(10)
9	(12)	(13)

Page 3

1)

+	5	6
4	(9)	(10)
6	(11)	(12)

2)

+	3	4
5	(8)	(9)
8	(11)	(12)

3)

+	4	7
2	(6)	(9)
7	(11)	(14)

4)

+	7	9
0	(7)	(9)
5	(12)	(14)

5)

+	8	9
4	(12)	(13)
7	(15)	(16)

6)

+	0	10
8	(8)	(18)
9	(9)	(19)

Page 4

1)

+	10	11
7	(17)	(18)
9	(19)	(20)

2)

+	5	8
10	(15)	(18)
11	(16)	(19)

3)

+	6	7
10	(16)	(17)
12	(18)	(19)

4)

+	10	14
3	(13)	(17)
5	(15)	(19)

5)

+	2	3
3	(5)	(6)
13	(15)	(16)

6)

+	4	5
6	(10)	(11)
16	(20)	(21)

Teacher Notes: pages 5-7

The inside numbers have the same pattern as the outside numbers, across and down. Using this pattern is a good way to check your answers.

Teacher Notes: page 8

The * indicates one possible starting place for each problem. In some cases, you could start in several places.

Page 5

1)

+	14	15
5	(19)	(20)
6	(20)	(21)

2)

+	7	9
19	(26)	(28)
20	(27)	(29)

3)

+	9	10
17	(26)	(27)
20	(29)	(30)

4)

+	10	11
10	(20)	(21)
11	(21)	(22)

5)

+	18	28
14	(32)	(42)
24	(42)	(52)

6)

+	13	23
8	(21)	(31)
38	(51)	(61)

Page 6

1)

+	(2)	(4)
4	6	8
10	(12)	(14)

2)

+	(1)	(8)
3	(4)	(11)
6	7	14

3)

+	(6)	(9)
0	6	9
5	(11)	(14)

4)

+	(3)	(8)
0	(3)	(8)
9	12	17

5)

+	(0)	(4)
4	(4)	(8)
7	7	11

6)

+	(3)	(4)
10	13	14
11	(14)	(15)

Page 7

1)

+	5	6
(2)	(7)	8
(3)	(8)	9

2)

+	3	5
(4)	7	(9)
(6)	9	(11)

3)

+	1	2
(8)	(9)	10
(9)	(10)	11

4)

+	6	8
(5)	11	(13)
(8)	14	(16)

5)

+	2	5
(5)	7	(10)
(8)	10	(13)

6)

+	5	6
(5)	(10)	11
(9)	(14)	15

Page 8

1)

+	5	(7)
0	*(5)	7
2	(7)	(9)

2)

+	4	(8)
2	*(6)	10
6	(10)	(14)

3)

+	*(6)	8
5	11	(13)
7	(13)	(15)

4)

+	*(5)	7
4	9	(11)
9	(14)	(16)

5)

+	6	(9)
3	*(9)	12
10	(16)	(19)

6)

+	*(4)	9
7	11	(16)
10	(14)	(19)

Puzzle Tables © 1980
Cuisenaire Company of America, Inc.

Teacher Notes: pages 9-11

   The * indicates one possible starting place for each problem. In some cases, you can start in several places.

Teacher Notes: page 12

   While there is only one correct inside number, there are many possible outside numbers.

Page 9

1)
+	5	9
4	9	13
7	12	16

2)
+	3	9
4	7	13
9	12	18

3)
+	3	5
5	8	10
7	10	12

4)
+	2	9
2	4	11
6	8	15

5)
+	0	5
6	6	11
9	9	14

6)
+	8	9
7	15	16
9	17	18

Page 10

1)
+	4	6
3	7	9
5	9	11

2)
+	1	4
1	2	5
7	8	11

3)
+	3	4
2	5	6
5	8	9

4)
+	1	3
4	5	7
8	9	11

5)
+	2	9
2	4	11
6	8	15

6)
+	5	8
2	7	10
3	8	11

Page 11

1)
+	4	10
5	9	15
7	11	17

2)
+	7	8
6	13	14
2	9	10

3)
+	8	10
1	9	11
2	10	12

4)
+	3	7
3	6	10
5	8	12

5)
+	8	16
5	13	21
15	23	31

6)
+	2	22
21	23	43
31	33	53

Page 12

1)
+		
	10	12
	16	18

2)
+		
	8	11
	13	16

3)
+		
	6	10
	8	12

4)
+		
	9	13
	15	19

5)
+		
	5	14
	15	24

6)
+		
	20	24
	36	40

Teacher Notes: page 13
  The inside numbers don't have the same pattern as the outside numbers. One way of correcting each of these is shown. There is more than one possible way.
Teacher Notes: page 14
  One possible answer is given for each problem.
Teacher Notes: page 16
  The inside numbers have the same difference as the outside numbers, across and down.

Page 13

1)
+	◯	◯
8	12	14
10	14	~~18~~ 16

2)
+	◯	◯
◯	7	10
◯	~~9~~ 8	11

3)
+	5	9
◯	~~11~~ 10	15
◯	13	18

4)
+	4	7
◯	11	◯
◯	13	~~15~~ 16

5)
+	◯	◯
◯	16	20
◯	21	~~27~~ 25

6) Make an impossible one of your own.
+		

Page 14

1)
+	①	③
②	3	5
③	4	6

2)
+	3	⑥
7	⑩	⑬
8	⑪	⑭

3)
+	③	⑤
4	⑦	⑨
7	⑩	12

4)
+	①	③
③	4	6
⑨	10	12

5)
+	②	④
③	5	7
⑦	9	11

6) Make up one of your own that has several answers.
+		

Page 15

1)
+	⑤	9
2	⑦	⑪
③	8	12
✔ Exactly one way

2)
+	②	⑥
2	4	8
⑥	8	16
✔ Impossible

3)
+	◯	⑧
3	◯	11
7	◯	⑮
✔ Several answers

4)
+	◯	◯
◯	4	6
◯	7	9
✔ Several answers

5)
+	◯	◯
◯	9	12
◯	10	14
✔ Impossible

6)
+	3	5
⓪	③	5
7	⑩	⑫
✔ Exactly one way

Page 16

1)
−	1	2
4	3	2
5	4	③

2)
÷	3	4
6	3	②
8	5	4

3)
−	1	5
7	6	2
9	⑧	4

4)
−	2	4
5	③	1
7	5	3

5)
−	6	7
8	2	1
10	④	③

6)
−	2	5
6	4	①
10	8	⑤

Page 52

Teacher Notes: pages 17-18
The inside numbers have the same difference as the outside numbers, across and down.

Teacher Notes: pages 19-20
The * indicates one possible starting place for each problem. In some cases, you could start in more than one place.

Page 17

1)

−	1	4
8	(7)	(4)
10	(9)	(6)

2)

−	2	6
9	(7)	(3)
12	(10)	6

3)

−	3	4
12	(9)	8
14	(11)	(10)

4)

−	6	9
14	(8)	(5)
16	10	(7)

5)

−	8	9
15	(7)	(6)
17	(9)	8

6)

−	6	7
13	7	(6)
15	(9)	(8)

Page 18

1)

−	4	7
11	(7)	(4)
15	(11)	(8)

2)

−	5	7
14	(9)	(7)
17	(12)	(10)

3)

−	5	9
9	(4)	(0)
19	(14)	(10)

4)

−	4	8
12	(8)	(4)
18	(14)	(10)

5)

−	7	8
10	(3)	(2)
16	(9)	(8)

6)

−	6	9
13	(7)	(4)
17	(11)	(8)

Page 19

1)

−	*(2)	(5)
8	6	3
10	(8)	(5)

2)

−	*(1)	(6)
7	(6)	(1)
9	8	3

3)

−	*(4)	(5)
5	1	0
9	(5)	(4)

4)

−	*(3)	(4)
8	(5)	(4)
12	9	8

5)

−	*(6)	(8)
11	(5)	(3)
15	9	7

6)

−	*(5)	(7)
12	7	5
16	(11)	(9)

Page 20

1)

−	1	2
*(3)	(2)	1
(5)	(4)	3

2)

−	3	4
*(5)	2	(1)
(9)	6	(5)

3)

−	2	5
*(7)	(5)	2
(8)	(6)	3

4)

−	4	5
*(6)	2	(1)
(10)	6	(5)

5)

−	3	6
*(7)	4	(1)
(9)	6	(3)

6)

−	3	4
*(4)	(1)	0
(10)	(7)	6

The * indicates one possible starting place for each problem. In some cases, you could start in more than one place.

Page 21

1)
−	(4)	8
13	9	5
17	(13)	(9)

2)
−	7	9
16	(9)	7
18	(11)	9

3)
−	(7)	(8)
11	(4)	(3)
15	8	7

4)
−	8	9
12	4	(3)
14	(6)	(5)

5)
−	7	9
18	(11)	9
19	(12)	10

6)
−	(6)	(8)
14	8	6
16	(10)	(8)

Page 22

1)
−	1	(3)
4	(3)	1
7	(6)	(4)

2)
−	0	(1)
2	(2)	1
6	(6)	(5)

3)
−	(0)	1
5	5	(4)
8	(8)	(7)

4)
−	(2)	5
6	4	(1)
7	(5)	(2)

5)
−	2	(4)
5	(3)	1
9	(7)	(5)

6)
−	(4)	6
8	4	(2)
10	(6)	(4)

Page 23

1)
−	4	5
(7)	3	(2)
10	(6)	(5)

2)
−	6	7
9	(3)	(2)
(12)	6	(5)

3)
−	6	7
(11)	(5)	4
15	(9)	(8)

4)
−	8	9
11	(3)	(2)
(15)	(7)	6

5)
−	(8)	9
16	8	(7)
19	(11)	(10)

6)
−	7	(8)
14	(7)	6
17	(10)	(9)

Page 24

1)
−	(6)	8
11	(5)	(3)
(14)	8	6

2)
−	(7)	9
(15)	8	(6)
19	12	(10)

3)
−	(7)	(8)
(15)	8	7
16	(9)	8

4)
−	6	8
(12)	6	4
(17)	11	(9)

5)
−	(5)	7
11	(6)	(4)
(19)	14	12

6)
−	8	(9)
(18)	(10)	9
(19)	11	10

Teacher Notes: page 25
  While there is only one correct inside number, there are many possible outside numbers.
Teacher Notes: page 26
  The inside numbers don't have the correct patterns. One way of correcting each of these is shown. There is more than one possible way.
Teacher Notes: page 27
  One possible answer is given for each problem.
Teacher Notes: page 28
  Each row and column of inside numbers has a common divisor. It is the outside number in that row or column.

Page 25

1)
(4)	2
7	5

2)
7	(4)
9	6

3)
5	2
8	(5)

4)
6	1
(10)	5

5)
6	(0)
7	1

6)
(4)	0
9	5

Page 26

1)
	○	○
8	5	2
9	6	~~4~~ 3

2)
	○	○
	4	3
○	~~7~~ 5	4

3)
	8	○
○	3	6
○	9	~~6~~ 12

4)
	5	9
○	6	~~1~~ 2
○	○	4

5)
	○	○
○	4	~~1~~ 2
○	7	5

6) Make an impossible one of your own.

Page 27

1)
	2	(3)
4	(2)	(1)
7	(5)	(4)

2)
	(5)	(6)
(7)	2	1
(8)	3	2

3)
	(1)	(2)
(5)	4	3
(7)	6	5

4)
	(6)	(9)
10	(4)	(1)
12	(6)	3

5)
	7	9
(13)	(6)	4
(10)	(3)	(1)

6) Make up one of your own that has several answers.

Page 28

1)
x	2	5
1	2	5
3	6	(15)

2)
x	1	4
2	2	(8)
5	5	20

3)
x	3	5
2	6	10
4	(12)	20

4)
x	2	4
3	(6)	12
4	8	16

5)
x	3	5
3	9	15
5	(15)	(25)

6)
x	0	4
2	0	(8)
5	0	(20)

Teacher Notes: pages 29-30
Each row and column of inside numbers has a common divisor. It is the outside number in that row or column.

Teacher Notes: pages 31-32
The * indicates one possible starting place for each problem. In some cases, you could start in more than one place.

Page 29

1)

x	5	6
2	10	(12)
3	(15)	(18)

2)

x	7	9
4	(28)	(36)
5	(35)	45

3)

x	7	8
3	(21)	24
6	(42)	(48)

4)

x	8	9
2	(16)	(18)
5	40	(45)

5)

x	4	6
1	(4)	(6)
7	(28)	42

6)

x	4	6
6	24	(36)
8	(32)	(48)

Page 30

1)

x	6	7
6	(36)	(42)
8	(48)	(56)

2)

x	6	7
5	(30)	(35)
7	(42)	(49)

3)

x	8	9
5	(40)	(45)
6	(48)	(54)

4)

x	7	8
7	(49)	(56)
8	(56)	(64)

5)

x	7	10
6	(42)	(60)
9	(63)	(90)

6)

x	5	9
7	(35)	(63)
9	(45)	(81)

Page 31

*

1)

x	(2)	(4)
4	8	16
10	(20)	(40)

*

2)

x	(1)	(8)
3	(3)	(24)
6	6	48

*

3)

x	(0)	9
0	0	0
5	(0)	45

*

4)

x	(4)	6
8	(32)	(48)
10	40	60

*

5)

x	(4)	9
7	(28)	(63)
8	32	72

*

6)

x	(7)	(10)
2	14	20
10	(70)	(100)

Page 32

1)

x	5	6
*(2)	(10)	12
(3)	(15)	18

2)

x	3	5
*(4)	12	(20)
(6)	18	(30)

3)

x	1	2
*(8)	(8)	16
(9)	(9)	18

4)

x	6	8
*(5)	30	(40)
(8)	48	(64)

5)

x	2	5
*(5)	10	(25)
(8)	16	(40)

6)

x	5	6
*(5)	(25)	30
(9)	(45)	54

Puzzle Tables © 1980
Cuisenaire Company of America, Inc.

The * indicates one possible starting place for each problem. In some cases, you could start in more than one place. On page 34, there is more than one correct answer for problem 2.

Page 33

1)
x	2	4
4	8	16
10	20	40

2)
x	1	8
3	3	24
6	6	48

3)
x	6	9
0	0	0
5	30	45

4)
x	3	8
0	0	0
9	27	72

5)
x	0	4
4	0	16
7	0	28

6)
x	3	4
9	27	36
10	30	40

Page 34

1)
x	4	8
2	8	16
6	24	48

2)
x	5	
0	0	0
2	10	

3)
x	6	8
5	30	40
7	42	56

4)
x	5	7
4	20	28
9	45	63

5)
x	6	9
3	18	27
10	60	90

6)
x	4	9
7	28	63
10	40	90

Page 35

1)
x	5	9
4	20	36
7	35	63

2)
x	3	9
4	12	36
9	27	81

3)
x	3	5
5	15	25
7	21	35

4)
x	2	9
2	4	18
6	12	54

5)
x	0	5
6	0	30
9	0	45

6)
x	8	9
7	56	63
9	72	81

Page 36

1)
x	4	6
3	12	18
5	20	30

2)
x	1	4
1	1	4
7	7	28

3)
x	3	4
2	6	8
5	15	20

4)
x	1	3
4	4	12
8	8	24

5)
x	2	9
2	4	18
6	12	54

6)
x	5	8
2	10	16
3	15	24

Teacher Notes: page 37
   While there is only one correct inside number, there may be more than one set of outside numbers.

Teacher Notes: page 39
   For problems 3 and 4, there could be any number of answers.

Page 37

1)

×		
	(6)	18
	10	30

2)

×		
	12	(28)
	27	63

3)

×		
	10	12
	15	(18)

4)

×		
	20	25
	(40)	50

5)

×		
	28	(32)
	42	48

6)

×		
	(42)	63
	48	72

Page 38

1)

×	(3)	(5)
9	27	45
(10)	(30)	50

☛ Exactly one way

2)

×	4	7
(5)	20	28
6	(24)	(42)

☑ Impossible

3)

×	(3)	(10)
4	12	40
( )	( )	( )

☛ Several answers

4)

×	(3)	(4)
(4)	12	16
(8)	24	36

☑ Impossible

5)

×	(4)	(6)
4	20	(24)
7	28	42

☛ Impossible

6)

×	6	( )
7	(42)	( )
9	(54)	( )

☛ Several answers

Page 39

1)

×	(1)	(2)
(4)	4	8
(5)	5	9

☑ Impossible

2)

×	( )	( )
( )	4	12
( )	6	18

☛ Several answers

3)

×	( )	( )
( )	( )	( )
( )	15	45

☛ Several answers

4)

×	7	( )
3	(21)	( )
4	(28)	( )

☑ Several answers

5)

×	(1)	(4)
(5)	5	20
(6)	6	(24)

☛ Exactly one way

6)

×	( )	( )
( )	24	36
( )	36	54

☛ Several answers

Page 40

1)

+	6	7
(5)	(11)	12
(7)	(13)	14

2)

−	(5)	(8)
10	(5)	(2)
15	10	7

3)

×	(6)	(7)
5	30	35
7	(42)	(49)

4)

−	6	9
(13)	7	(4)
(18)	12	(9)

5)

×	5	8
(4)	20	(32)
(9)	45	(72)

6)

+	5	8
(4)	(9)	12
(9)	(14)	17

Puzzle Tables © 1980
Cuisenaire Company of America, Inc.

Page 41

1)

×	7	9
(6)	(42)	54
(8)	(56)	72

2)

−	(4)	(7)
11	7	4
14	(10)	(7)

3)

+	7	9
(6)	13	(15)
(8)	15	(17)

4)

−	8	9
(12)	(4)	3
(17)	9	8

5)

+	(8)	(9)
5	13	14
8	(16)	(17)

6)

×	(8)	(9)
5	(40)	(45)
8	64	72

Page 42

1)

−	3	7
(9)	6	(2)
11	(8)	(4)

2)

×	(6)	7
3	(18)	(21)
8	48	(56)

3)

+	1	(4)
5	(6)	9
9	(10)	(13)

4)

−	(8)	9
11	3	(2)
14	(6)	(5)

5)

×	(8)	9
5	40	(45)
6	(48)	(54)

6)

+	8	9
(3)	(11)	12
7	(15)	(16)

Page 43

1)

+	(5)	6
2	7	(8)
4	(9)	(10)

2)

×	3	7
4	(12)	(28)
(7)	21	(49)

3)

−	8	9
(17)	(9)	8
19	(11)	(10)

4)

+	3	7
6	(9)	(13)
(8)	11	(15)

5)

−	7	(9)
16	(9)	7
18	(11)	(9)

6)

×	8	9
(7)	56	(63)
8	(64)	(72)

Page 44

1)
T

(LxT)+2	7	10
L 4	30	(42)
5	(37)	(52)

2)

(L+T)+10	3	6
4	(17)	(20)
7	(20)	23

3)

(LxT)-5	10	12
6	(55)	(67)
8	75	(91)

4)

(L+T)x2	2	5
3	(10)	(16)
4	12	(18)

5)

(2xL)+T	2	3
5	12	(13)
9	(20)	(21)

6) Make up one of your own.

1) (L+T)x5

	(1)	3
(0)	(5)	15
7	40	(50)

Add the left number and the top number and then multiply the result by 5.

2) (LxT)+1

	4	(7)
6	(25)	43
(9)	37	(64)

Multiply the left number and the top number and then add 1.

3) (L+2)+T

	(6)	(10)
7	15	19
12	(20)	(24)

Add 2 to the left number and then add the top number.

4) (2xL)+T

	2	4
5	(12)	14
(7)	16	(18)

Multiply the left number by 2 and then add the top number.

5) (2xL)-T

	(2)	4
5	8	(6)
(7)	(12)	10

Multiply the left number by 2 and then subtract the top number.

6) Make up one of your own.

1) (L+T)-6

	7	8
10	(11)	(12)
11	12	(13)

Add the left number and the top number and then subtract 6.

2) (L+1)xT

	9	15
4	45	(75)
5	(54)	(90)

Add 1 to the left number and then multiply the result by the top number.

3) (L+T)²

	4	10
3	49	(256)
5	(81)	(225)

Add the left number and the top number and then square their sum.

4) L²+T

	4	10
6	(40)	(46)
7	53	(59)

Square the left number and then add the top number.

5) L+T²

	4	10
6	22	(106)
7	(23)	(107)

Square the top number and then add the left number.

6) Make up one of your own.

1) (L+T)+5

	9	11
4	18	20
5	19	21

Add the left number and the top number and then add 5.

2) (2xL)-T

	12	13
7	2	1
10	8	7

Multiply the left number by 2 and then subtract the top number.

3) (2xL)+T

	5	7
0	5	7
3	11	13

Multiply the left number by 2 and then add the top number.

4) Lx(T-1)

	7	8
10	60	70
12	72	84

Subtract 1 from the top number and then multiply the result by the left number.

5) L+(2xT)

	4	7
8	16	22
9	17	23

Multiply the top number by 2 and then add the left number.

6) Make up one of your own.

Teacher Notes: page 48

The black-line master can be used in many ways. Teachers and students may use it as a master to make up their own worksheets. Students may use it as a recording sheet for problems with more than one possible answer. Teachers may use it to produce other masters with certain numbers missing.